BRIGHT IDEA BOOKS

YOU CAN WORK ON Broadway

by Samantha S. Bell

CAPSTONE PRESS
a capstone imprint

Bright Idea Books are published by Capstone Press
1710 Roe Crest Drive, North Mankato, Minnesota 56003
www.mycapstone.com

Library of Congress Cataloging-in-Publication Data
Library of Congress Cataloging-in-Publication Data is available on the Library of Congress website.
ISBN: 978-1-5435-4144-1 (library hardcover)
ISBN: 978-1-5435-4184-7 (eBook PDF)

Editorial Credits
Editor: Charly Haley
Designer: Becky Daum
Production Specialist: Claire Vanden Branden

Photo Credits
iStockphoto: ferrantraite, 15, Steve Debenport, 26-27; Shutterstock Images: A_Lesik, 20-21, Andrey Petrovas, cover (foreground), 29, Chris Cornish, 24-25, Christian Bertrand, 16-17, Dean Drobot, 6-7, dibrova, 8-9, Igor Bulgarin, 19, 30-31, Kozlik, cover (background), 11, 23, Pavel L Photo and Video, 5, Rommel Canlas, 12

Design Elements: iStockphoto, Red Line Editorial, and Shutterstock Images

TABLE OF CONTENTS

CHAPTER 1

PRODUCERS

An actor speaks onstage. Other actors join him. They sing and dance. They wear costumes. It's a Broadway show!

Broadway is a famous street in New York City. There are many theaters on that street. Broadway theaters are among the best in the world. Some Broadway plays are **musicals**.

Many different people work in theater. It takes a lot of people to put on a show. They all work together. They want to make the show the best it can be.

Broadway shows often have many actors.

It all starts with the **producer**. Producers read play **scripts**. They choose a play. They get the money to put on the show.

The producer chooses the **director**. They work together. They work with the music director too.

People who write scripts want producers to read their work. They want producers to make their scripts into plays.

Broadway shows are famously advertised in New York City's Times Square.

Producers also **advertise** their plays. They tell people to watch shows at the theater.

Producers need to be good leaders. They must work well with other people. Most go to college. They may study writing or acting.

CHAPTER 2

CAST Members

The people who are in a play are called cast members. They can be actors and singers. They may be dancers. Most must try out for their **roles**.

Actors spend hours onstage during a show. They may have a lot of **lines**.

HAIR AND MAKEUP ARTISTS

Hair and makeup artists are important too. They make actors look like the characters in the play.

Actors wear costumes when they perform.

Cast members practice the show many times. They must get ready to perform in front of people. This is called **rehearsing**.

When actors start rehearsing a new play, they read the script.

Cast members may get nervous before a show. But they learn to stay calm. They perform with a lot of energy. They may do eight shows in one week!

Some actors go to college. Some start acting in high school plays. Others act in small theaters.

CHAPTER 3

DIRECTORS

Directors guide everyone who works on a play. Directors help show the story on the stage. They want people to understand the story.

Directors make sure everyone works together.

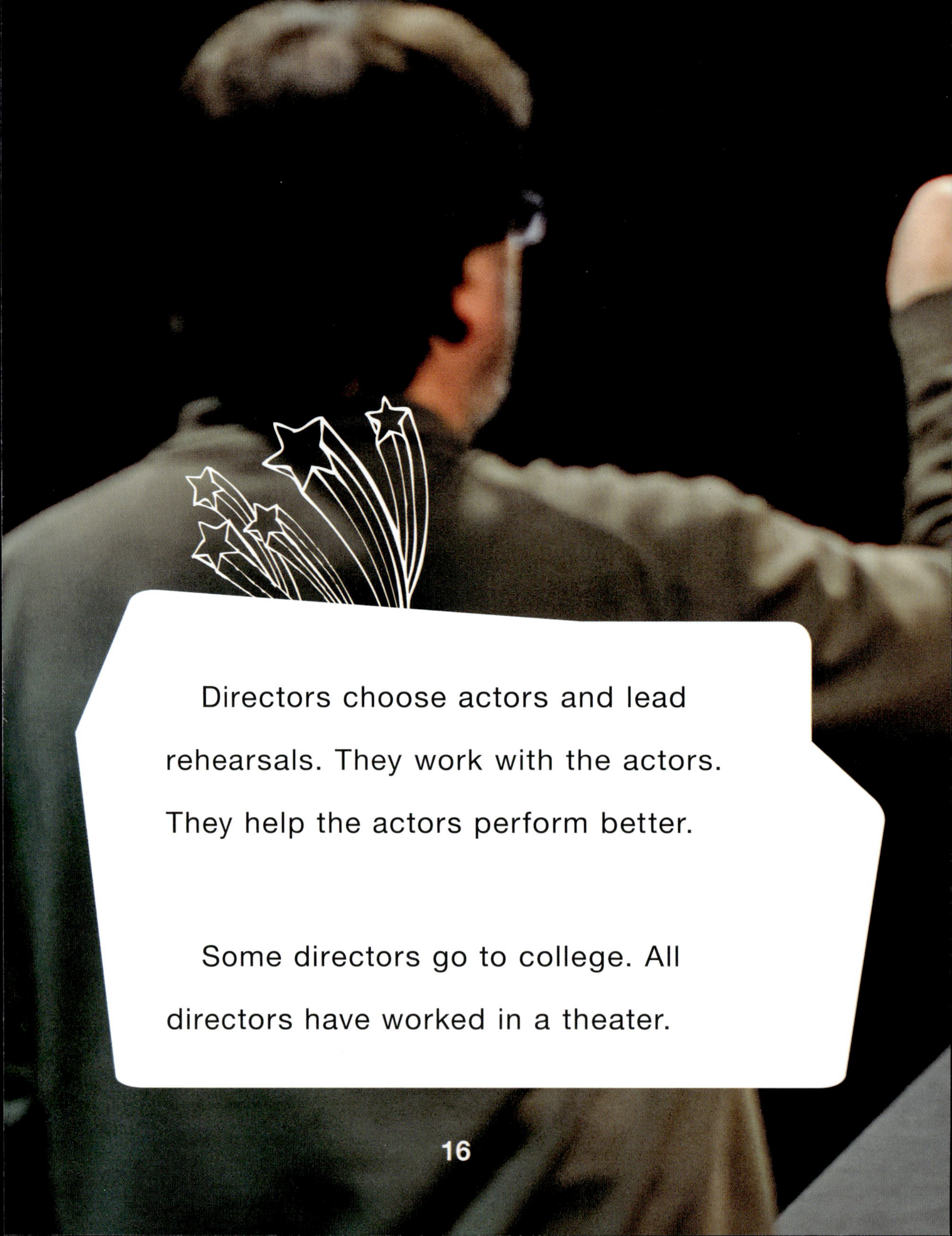

Directors choose actors and lead rehearsals. They work with the actors. They help the actors perform better.

Some directors go to college. All directors have worked in a theater.

A director sometimes works with one actor at a time.

CHAPTER 4

MUSIC Directors

Music directors organize the music for plays. They help the musicians and actors learn songs.

CHOREOGRAPHERS

Choreographers create dances for the show. They listen to the music and songs. They think about the story. They want the dances to look good.

In Broadway musicals, actors sing and dance to music.

Orchestras are usually in front of the stage.

Most Broadway plays have an **orchestra**. The orchestra has many musicians. They play music for the show.

The music director **conducts** the show. This helps all musicians know when to play. It helps them sound good together.

Some music directors go to college. They often start by working as musicians.

CHAPTER 5

STAGE Managers

Stage **managers** make sure the show runs smoothly. Most stage managers are part of a team. They take turns doing many jobs.

Stage managers plan rehearsals. They keep track of costumes and **props**.

COSTUME AND SET DESIGNERS

Costume designers choose what actors wear. They make actors look like their characters. Set designers make the play's setting on the stage. They might build a fake house for the actors.

Sets, props, and costumes help a play come to life.

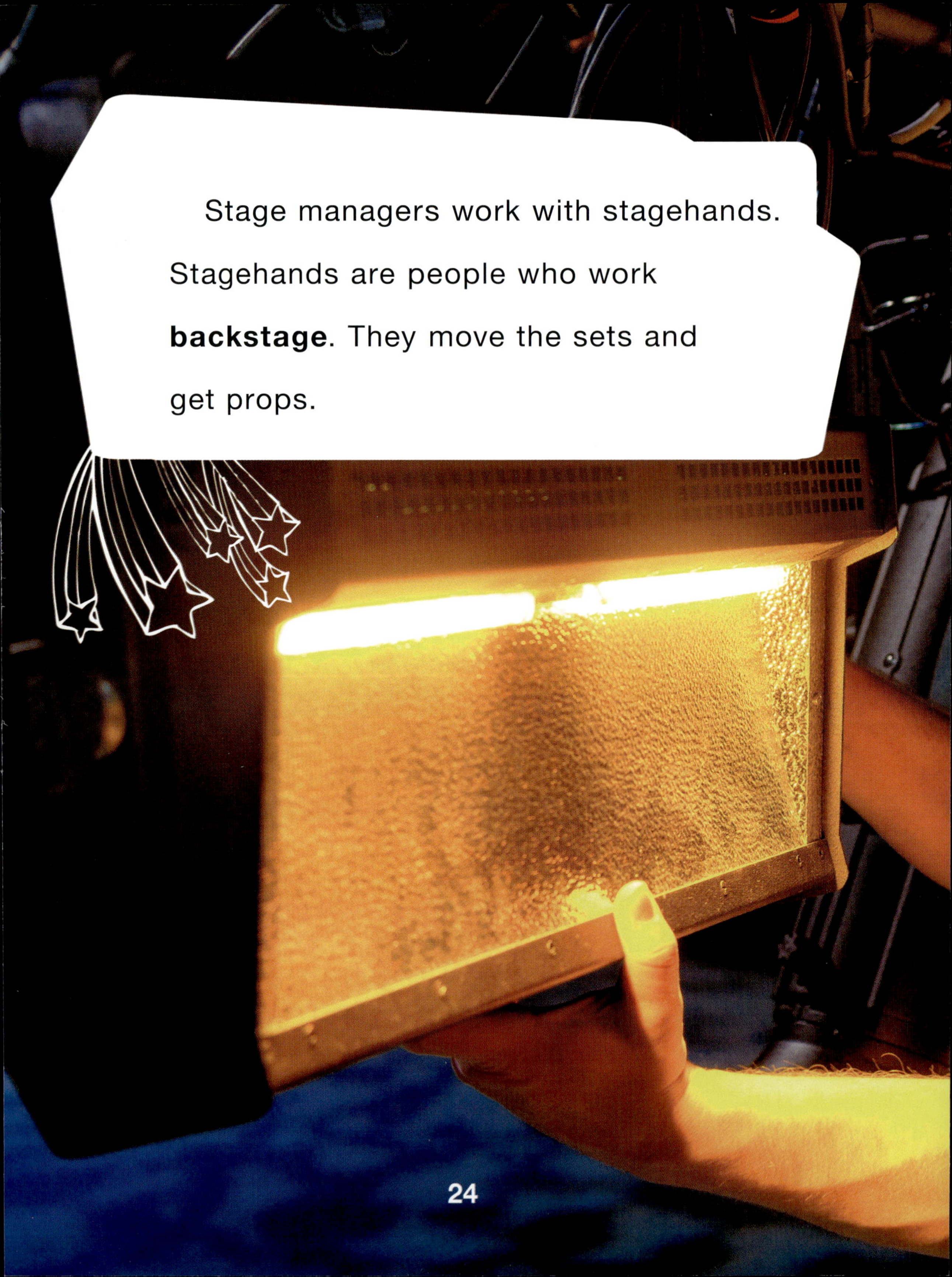

Stage managers work with stagehands. Stagehands are people who work **backstage**. They move the sets and get props.

People backstage run lights and sound for plays.

Do you dream of performing onstage or working backstage? You might like to work on Broadway!

Stage managers give **cues** during shows. A cue might tell an actor when to go onstage. There are also cues for lights and sound. Most shows have hundreds of cues.

Stage managers deal with problems during a show. They make sure everything works right. They help if an actor is hurt.

Some stage managers go to college. Others do not. They all have worked backstage.

GLOSSARY

advertise
to tell people about something that is being sold

backstage
behind the stage of a theater

choreographer
a person who makes dance routines

conduct
to direct singers or musicians

cue
a signal for someone to do something

director
a person who is in charge of actors and crew members

lines
parts of the script that the actors say out loud

manager
a person who is in charge of a project or organization

musical
a play that tells a story with songs

orchestra
a group of musicians who play many different instruments

producer
a person who manages money and other parts of making a play

prop
an object used by actors in a show

rehearse
to practice a play

role
the character played by an actor

script
the written form of a play including lines for actors

FURTHER RESOURCES

Do you want to learn more about Broadway? Check out these books and websites:

Broadway.org: Find out if a Broadway show is coming to your city
https://www.broadway.org/tours

Hosein, Ann. *The History of Theatre*. New York: Britannica Educational Publishing in association with Rosen Educational Services, 2016.

PBS: "Broadway or Bust"
http://www.pbs.org/wgbh/broadway-or-bust

Vescia, Monique. *Choose Your Own Career Adventure on Broadway*. Ann Arbor, Mich.: Cherry Lake Publishers, 2016.

Are you interested in the story of someone who works on Broadway? Check out this book:

Schwartz, Heather E. *Idina Menzel: Vocal Superpower*. Minneapolis, Minn.: Lerner Publications, 2015.

ACTIVITY

PUT ON A SHOW!

Ask a parent or teacher to help you find Broadway songs online. Choose your favorite one and learn the words. Next, decide if you will add dancing. Listen to the music. Create a dance. Decide what costume you will wear. Finally, call your family or friends together to watch your show!

INDEX